Meditations and Devotions for Adults

Alec J. Langford

Alec J. Langford

ABINGDON Nashville

Meditations and Devotions for Adults

Acknowledgment is made to the following publications for permission to reprint meditations and prayers:

The Christian, published by the Christian Board of Publication, St. Louis, Missouri, for Prayer (unsigned), "The Shepherd," "Lord, I Shall be verie busy this day," "Meditation on Confession—*Potacion of Lent,*" and "Hold on Tightly."

The Disciple, published by the Christian Board of Publication, St. Louis, Missouri, for "You've Got Two Hands, Why Don't You Use Them?"

Sunshine Magazine, published by Sunshine Press, for Power."

Vanguard magazine, for "Lent."

Quotation from "Look Wider Still," copyright © 1963 Girl Scouts of the U.S.A., words and music by Fred L. Todd, used by permission. Poem by David MacLenon is reprinted with the permission of *Church Management.* Excerpt from Earl Wilson, *Indianapolis Star,* is reprinted with permission. Quotation from "Barter" from the *Collected Poems* of Sara Teasdale, printed with permission of Macmillan Publishing Co., Inc. Copyright 1917 by Macmillan Publishing Co., Inc., renewed 1945 by Mamie T. Wheless.

Scripture quotations noted RSV are from the Revised Standard Version of the Bible, copyright 1946, 1952, and 1971 by the Division of Christian Education, National Council of Churches, and are used by permission. Scripture quotations noted NEB are from the New English Bible, copyright © the Delegates of the Oxford University Press 1961, 1970. Reprinted by permission. One scripture quotation is from Today's English Version of the New Testament. Copyright © American Bible Society 1966.

Library of Congress Cataloging in Publication Data

Langford, Alec J   1926-
    Meditations and devotions for adults.
    1. Meditations. I. Title.
    BV4832.2.L317   242'.6'4   76-223

ISBN 0-687-24090-5

MANUFACTURED BY THE PARTHENON PRESS AT NASHVILLE, TENNESSEE, UNITED STATES OF AMERICA

to my wife Alice

whose suggestions and selections
helped to make this a book

Contents

NEW YEAR

Get ready for the new year.
Get ready for the year 2000.
Get ready for the twenty-first century!

There's a new world coming; are we ready for it? For that matter are we ready for the year which has just begun? There's always the question of whether we are "up with," "abreast of" the time for which we have been called. Sometimes we feel very much out of step with the time, ahead maybe or behind, but certainly not in step. It's not always easy to know what is the beat of the time. Some presidents don't know it, some dictators and kings haven't known it, so I suppose it's not so inexcusable for us commoners to fail to grasp the mood and meaning and potential of the times.

> Some feel they have been educated for the wrong
> profession—they can't get a job.
> Some feel they have spent their life in the wrong field
> —they find their specialty turns into a dodo bird.
> Some know they have invested in the wrong stocks
> —they turned down a winner and invested in a
> loser.

I feel particularly sorry for the person who seems to be out of step with everything that is happening. A loser born, he doesn't like the political climate; he doesn't agree with technological progress; he can't stand pop music or modern art; he finds fashion shameful or scandalous; and, to top it all off, he claims there is nothing good in religion. Fortunately most of us react to some things positively, we are neutral about others, and to some we are negative. A mixed reaction is good.

> To take everything in the world as good is to be nauseatingly sentimental.
> To be neutral about everything is to contribute nothing.
> To be negative about everything is to be sick.
> Now the question—Are you ready for the new year?

Suggested Bible Reading: *Hebrews 12:1-17*

Prayer:
O God, whose name is great, wonderful and holy, grant that we and all thy children may glorify thee, not only with our lips, but with our lives. In so far as our past thoughts, words, and acts have reflected thy will, we pray that thou wilt set the seal of thine approval upon them, and where we have hindered thy purposes, we ask thy forgiveness. Free us from enslavement to pessimistic predictions and from past failures. When we hesitate because of uncertainty or fear, rekindle in us the confidence that thou art working in everything for the good. Amen.

LIFE

It is a pity some of the gems of wit and wisdom so generously shared in a barber shop are wasted on such a limited audience! Here is one heard recently that can be shared.

An employee at a large manufacturing plant was operating a machine that puts threads on axles. For some reason he wanted to speed up production on the machine and so, made an adjustment to it. He made an adjustment all right! The next day it was discovered that he had spent a whole shift cutting rings around steel shafts instead of threads.

The result—

(1) a great pile of useless steel pieces;
(2) a dismissed straw boss;
(3) a reprimanded employee;
(4) axle shafts that had to be cut off, welded, and machined again.

Life, like the thread-cutting machine, can seem to go unattended for periods of time; what with the power on, the operator present, the materials at hand, and the correct dies in place, everything seems to be working. Wheels turn, fluid pours down to aid in cutting and cooling the cutting tool, and, as almost final evidence that a perfect job is being done, a great quantity of metal cuttings pile up.

A quick glance at a shaft allows only a skilled, alert operator to tell whether threads or circles are being made. There is a very small adjustment in some machines that makes the difference between cutting one or the other. There is also a very simple test to prove there is really a thread, and even a person with the most limited skill can do this.

Here are some of the additional comparisons we can make with life. It should be purposeful—threaded—not just full of circles. In the movement and noise it may not always be obvious whether threads or circles are being produced. It is always possible and relatively simple to be sure by checking against the "master" life.

Suggested Bible Reading: *Luke 7:1-14*

Prayer:
O God,
  Build,
  Etch,
  Tatoo,
  Paint,
  Print,
  Engrave in our minds the greatness of thy design. Amen.

CREATING OR WRECKING

Do you ever read the telephone directory? I do sometimes. Once I began reading from the back of the yellow pages. I had only turned one page when I came upon a subject for lengthy meditation—the advertisements of the wrecking contractors.

To begin, there were twenty-three of them listed, and that seemed plenty for a city of a million people. Just imagine twenty-three companies loose for a whole year: what a mess they could make! You've heard the joke about the wreckers who came and demolished the wrong house? It wasn't a joke!

As I went over their advertising blurb, I didn't think this was much of a joke either. One agency has over three hundred trucks to carry off the debris—it means business. Another had plenty of experience, having been at it twenty-one years. It claims seventy-three thousand buildings demolished. What a record!

Do you make anything of this? I make plenty. There is a "time to build," and, evidently, there is a time to wreck. Planned obsolescence is a part of our thinking and evidently is applied to our society from dime-store objects to the largest structure you can find. Some of this activity is reminiscent of the way children play with blocks; painstaking minutes are spent building a fancy tower or a house or a castle or a bridge, and then in a second, with a sweep of the hand, the whole thing becomes a meaningless heap.

If this were the end of the story, it would be rather tragic, but it is not. The clean sweep is made in order to begin again. Whether it is with a child's blocks or multi-story buildings covering blocks of land, the destruction is only a prelude to beginning again to build better or bigger or more permanently. An important consideration seems to be that we focus carefully on what is planned and that we be certain that we do not become wrapped up in the sheer joy of tearing down just to see what can be built again.

That same directory carried 226 building contractors— almost ten times the number of wreckers listed. As long as we have that balance we should be safe. There should be more building than breaking, more wrought than wrecked.

These thoughts are meant to extend beyond the physical aspect of building. They also apply to our way of dealing with the social institutions around us, and there is a very important way in which they apply to our personal relationships. Are we doing more wrecking, or more building?

Suggested Bible Reading: *Psalm 127*

Prayer:

O God, who didst make us in thy likeness, keep us from marring and disfiguring thy work. Help us to be content with the talent we possess and to rejoice with those who have great gifts. May the spirit of love displayed in our actions, reflect that love which is eternally in thy heart. Amen.

EVANGELISM

Consider the turtle.
He makes progress
Only when his neck is out.

This good old slogan may well have been thought up by some philosopher of the distant past who sat watching a turtle come out of a muddy lake. Its origin is uncertain but its message is clear.

We need people who will "stick their necks out" for a principle.
We need people who won't sit idle when wrongs need to be righted.
We need people who won't keep their heads in a shell when misstatements are made.
We need people who stand out rather than merge with the muddy landscape.

"Sticking your neck out" for what is right, takes courage. It takes much courage if what is right isn't popular. Woodrow Wilson said it this way, "It is just as hard to do your duty when men are sneering at you, as when they are shooting at you."

One specific sticking-your-neck-out project for Christians is evangelism. There are risks when evangelizing.

Outright rejection of your effort to communicate the gospel is one of them. Another risk is exposure to severe questioning that might threaten the evangelist's own beliefs. Yet the church must have people who are willing to "stick their necks out" to share their Christian faith.

Suggested Bible Reading: *John 4:26-42*

Prayer:
Let us pray:
> *for those being won to Christ and the church*
> *for those being reclaimed to a life of usefulness and purpose*
> *for those led to eager discipleship, giving themselves in new ways*
> *for those learning the faith, wrestling with doubts and questions*
> *for those experimenting with their Christianity*
> *for those sharing the good news.*

O God, we would seek to appreciate the many conditions and crises confronted by men. Keep us ever in touch with the striving, struggling, aspiring, hopeful ones and let us be ready and willing to share whatever hope and encouragement we have with those who lack these qualities. Amen.

SELF-PERSPECTIVE

"You will probably feel about 10 percent shorter for a few days," he explained, as he went through details of something that was going to affect my life from then on. Who welcomes the prospect of being 10 percent shorter?

There is such a thing as being brought down to size, and I presume we all do well to measure ourselves at times. In this I mean with something other than the traditional yardstick—measuring ourselves against reality or measuring ourselves against someone else's height, importance, or standing.

What the man did not fully explain in the interview was that others would appear larger. You see I was not facing an operation that cut six inches off each leg. I was in an optometrist's office being fitted with bifocals. To my surprise, when the new lenses arrived I found that I was seeing certain things not only sharper but larger than they had appeared before. Over the years, without realizing it, I had lost some acuity, some sharpness, some perspective, and now it was back again, I was living in a new world.

Taking a summer vacation, reading some books with fresh ideas, enrolling in a course at college, meeting some new people—there are many ways in which we can get a new perspective, a new vision of life. As time passes many people lose certain perspectives and need an opportunity to correct or improve their general outlook.

16

This is what the Christian is doing in the church—getting a new and corrected perspective of life. "When anyone is united to Christ, there is a new world; . . . a new order has already begun" (II Cor. 5:17 NEB).

Suggested Bible Reading: *Hebrews 2:5-9*

Prayer:
O God, the light, life and power of all creatures; we come to thee in humility because we are aware of thy greatness. May thy goodness make us love thee above all our human affections, thy power and justice make us revere thee above all that we owe in reverence or fear to any human person.

We thank thee for the many ways in which thou has been made known to us and for the opportunity, if we are willing, to come very close to thee in the common round of ordinary living.

In appreciation of thy changelessness we would strive to be more steadfast and consistent throughout our lives. Enable us to live up to the highest standard that we know. Give us sympathy for and consideration of those who appear unable to maintain their grasp on higher things.

Through Jesus Christ who shows us the victory over all selfishness, pride and sin, we take courage knowing that he was able to conquer all. Upon whatever path of life we tread, we pray that we may have thee as our unfailing guide. Amen.

HEAVEN—HOW TO GET THERE

Miracle Morris, a retail furniture salesman from Queens, attended $25,000 worth of events in 30 years by pretending he was invited. . . . Retired to West Palm Beach, . . . he winces at the term "gate-crashing." Morris simply attended without being asked, and what's so wrong about that? Maybe they forgot to invite him. Maybe the computer made a mistake!

That's the way Earl Wilson wrote about Morris Lieberman in a column. As a gate-crasher supreme he probably deserves a place in the *Guinness Book of Records*. The chronicle of his achievements is cause for amazement. Pictured with presidents and in conversation with celebrities, he knew the great and famous; he had met them, talked with them, drunk with them, dined with them— all without benefit of an official invitation or introduction.

Wilson continued, "Why did he go into semi-retirement? I suspect he is going to try to trick [his way] past the doorman at the Heavenly Velvet Rope, and if he fails, it will be the first time he has failed. The only difficulty as I see it, is that a card from the 'media' won't be accepted Up There at the Main Entrance!"

Now, perhaps you can see the way this story on Miracle Morris set me thinking. How many of us are trying to pull a "Miracle Morris" in the hopes of tricking our way past the doorman at the Heavenly Velvet Rope? Voting for the "right" thing, getting a name on a roll, attending a token number of church activities, getting named to a

18

committee, accepting a job in the church are just a few Miracle-Morris type tricks. We could go on and on, realizing that almost everyone is included somewhere in the subterfuge of trying to make himself more important, better than he is in reality.

While Miracle Morris has a message for us about how far you can go with a lot of gall, push, bluff, and self-assurance (a message we don't really need), we have a message for him. Miracle Morris doesn't need to scheme over ways of getting past the doorman at the Heavenly Velvet Rope. Up there it's Open House, and we presume no amount of trickery will get you in nor will lack of formal attire, authenticated invitation, or anything else keep you out, provided you are genuine.

Suggested Bible Reading: *Mark 10:17-27*

Prayer:
Eternal Father, thou art ever the same and thy love is constant. We see the task and the joy of continued growth in thy likeness. Every day we would attain some part of that divine ambition. Every day we would leave behind something of our imperfect life. May the passing weeks bring us assurance that our efforts are not in vain —that we are making progress toward the goal of all our striving, the measure of the stature of the fullness of Christ. Amen.

BURDENS

> The cross that he bore and
> the crown that he wore;
> these were his own.

While traveling in Mexico we noticed loads carried and arranged differently from those we usually see—

- a woman with a big bundle balanced on her head;
- a man with a sombrero (specially designed) packed full of parcels, plus bundles back and front on a bicycle;
- a boy with a three-wheeled bike carrying two huge chunks of ice and a younger boy riding along with him;
- a burro with a load of stalks so large that only his nose showed in front of this strange moving mass;
- a woman carrying a baby in her arms while progressing on her knees toward the shrine of Guadalupe;
- a couple of workmen carrying a bucket of gravel to the top of a pyramid to make repairs.

To me some of these loads seemed hard to carry—awkward, enormous, or even an outrage to the dignity of the person bearing the burden. In most instances the one carrying the load displayed no sign of being put-upon or overburdened. A small boy almost staggering under the load of the not-too-small burden on his back was offered sympathy by an observer. He responded pertly, "He is no burden, he's my brother!"

Perspective and attitude make a vast difference in the way we regard the load we carry whether it be of sticks or straw, bricks or baggage. The same applies to other burdens—those of responsibility, guilt, doubt, or worry.

In a passage in which Paul talks about carrying things he says this, "Help one another to carry these heavy loads, and in this way you will fulfil the law of Christ" (Gal. 6:2 NEB). We might write along beside it, "Keep alert to the fact that while you have a load to carry, others around you may be carrying awkward, cumbersome, embarrassing, difficult, or almost unbearable loads."

Suggested Bible Reading: *Galatians 6:1-10*

Prayer:
Father we thank thee that men of muscle, who toil through storms, who have to sweat for their living, who know the disappointment of coming home empty-handed can also know the exhilaration of following thy son. Help us to appreciate more fully the fact that the way of life Jesus demonstrated was both practical and attractive. As Peter found Christ to be a thrilling companion, may we also find him to be our most stimulating friend. Amen.

21

LAUGHTER

"Our ability to laugh is deteriorating," editorialized *Life* magazine as it sought to sum up the national situation in the early seventies. This point caught my eye because it was almost exactly what I was saying at the time. We are taking ourselves too seriously. Nothing is funny anymore.

I looked at the editor's statement carefully and read the words over again because he seemed to be careful in choosing them. He was not implying we should say Ha! Ha!, laugh at ourselves, laugh at others, smirk, get the last laugh; rather he was saying we need to be able to just laugh—laugh because life is good, laugh because there is joy in what we are doing, laugh because it gives others a lift.

A recent write-up of church activities that appeared in the local newspaper read: "There will be classes for children and a nursery for adults." Yes, that might be just what we need, a nursery for adults, staffed by clowns so that we can learn to be young again and laugh again. Was this what a certain person meant when he said, "Except you become as little children . . ."?

Suggested Bible Reading: *Genesis 17:15-22, 18:1-15*

Prayer:

> *Take possession of us, O God:*
> *Like a ship needs steering,*
> *Like a house needs to be lived in,*
> *Like a person needs to be loved.*
> *Take possession of us, we pray. Amen*

OBSERVATION

A lens dropped out of my glasses, right onto the pad on my desk. The optometrist couldn't repair the frame but ordered a new "chassis." It was supposed to arrive the next week.

In the meantime I carried on my usual activities with one lens in and one lens out. Those who were in church on Sunday were treated to a "one-eyed" sermon! Now what surprised me was that of the dozens of people who were around me, only one remarked about the missing lens. For a start I was so self-conscious about it I kept mentioning it; but when I called it to people's attention, they invariably said they had not noticed.

This reinforces an old lesson: You see what you expect to see—you hear what you expect to hear. On the one hand this causes us to miss a multitude of things every day of our lives; on the other hand it saves us from wasting our time and attention on thousands of routine details.

Sara Teasdale says this better in her poem "Barter":

> Life has loveliness to sell
> All beautiful and splendid things,
> Blue waves whitened on a cliff,
> Soaring fire that sways and sings,
> And children's faces looking up
> Holding wonder like a cup.

What have you noticed lately? Something missing, or something extra?

Suggested Bible Reading: *John 12:37-50*

Prayer:
Sometimes when we pray to thee, O God, we know afterwards that while our lips have been repeating words of compassion for the plight of others, our minds have failed to grasp the necessity for action which our hands must undertake to make this prayer become reality. O God, make us cautious when we pray, that we do not stop praying too soon. Let us pray with our lips and then continue our prayer with our hands.

Sometimes when we pray to thee, O God, we have closed our eyes and not only shut out the distraction of the movement around us, but have tried to remove ourselves from the world of reality to which, sooner or later, we must return. In these moments when we close our eyes to petty, incidental distractions, please God, help us to open our minds to the larger problems that face us as human beings. Let us confront undeserved and seemingly unavoidable suffering, selfishness and apparently insatiable greed, violence and the conditions that breed or cause warped minds.

Sometimes when we have prayed to thee, O God, we

have knelt or bowed our heads only to conform, only to share in the custom of those around us. Our conformity has been a disguise, for in reality we have felt like looking thee straight in the eye and telling thee how to handle humanity, how to work the world, and when to stop interfering. For this kind of insufferable pride we ask again to be forgiven. Amen.

PERSISTENCE

A great big hole in the ground
   cactus
      a huge industrial plant
         moments with Mr. Lincoln
       an atomic energy plant
      a home workshop
     red dirt
         the Hoover-Boulder Dam
        Molly the golfer

This may seem a strange assortment, but it happens to be a selection of things on which I made notes while on vacation one summer, things that sooner or later were likely to find their way into my writing or speaking.

In the Olympics of 1972 a runner fell flat on his back, got up, and ran on to win the race. Would he have won if he had not fallen? Sometimes an accident like that, which seems to make a goal impossible, is just the stimulus a person needs, though it is by no means the usual result.

A week or so earlier a similar illustration had been given to me by Molly the golfer. She said, "When I hit a ball and it goes in the water, I just get out another ball and hit it again. Some of the other women who play with me fold up when that happens to them and can't really play for the rest of the game. I go right on!"

She was really making a point about life—the kind of life she leads. You play with remainders in life itself.

How do you see yourself in the game of life? Playing it like Molly the golfer, getting up and running again like an Olympic runner, trying again and succeeding gloriously like Mark Spitz—this is one way. There is another—you can smash your clubs, get up and run in the wrong direction, and just throw in the towel. We are looking for more to join the ranks of those who persist, who go right on!

Suggested Bible Reading: *II Timothy 3:10-17*

Prayer:
As the sage of old worshiped thee, O God, and said "Lead me to the rock that is higher than I," may we, too, be led in our worship to that which is loftier than our level of thinking, higher than the height of our feeling, and nobler than the zenith of our striving. We come from cares and pleasures to take stock of the prevailing direction of our lives, to confess that we have taken many wrong roads, and to ask thee for directions for the days to come. In the name of the one who knew best how to order life and how to worship thee, even Jesus Christ. Amen.

CROWN OR CROSS

"Look! I've got a crown on my head!" Familiar words? The character in the margarine ad has a grin of satisfaction that rivals the grin on a Cheshire cat. Not only is history replete with information about the honor and glory of wearing a crown, literature as far down the line as a nursery rhyme adds an aura to crowns and being crowned. Remember the little tragedy in Jack and Jill?

"Jack fell down and broke his crown . . ."

Kings and queens who wear crowns are usually aware of a great load of responsibility placed on them. Even the more frivolous use of a crown for honoring a winner of a beauty contest sometimes sobers a winner into realizing that the publicity is a mixed blessing and that with the crown comes a responsibility to show an example and to reign with dignity. Shakespeare in the play *King Henry IV, Part II* says this for us in the line, "Uneasy lies the head that wears a crown."

Charles XII had the audacity to set the crown on his head at his coronation. We presume this was what caused Dag Hammarskjold to write: "The shamelessness of great pride: it lifts the crown from the cushion and places it upon its brow with its own hands." He continues with a fable: "Once upon a time, there was a crown so heavy that it could only be worn by one who remained completely oblivious to its glitter."

When crowns of opportunity are placed within our reach, we are all human enough to want to feel them, to lift them, to try them on for size. When crowns of power or prestige are placed at a tempting distance from us, we do well to remember one who was offered these things yet whose only crown was a wreath of thorns.

What kind of a crown have you been given? Is it one for beauty, for physical strength, for wealth, for leadership, for other status? Then wear it with care, wear it with caution. But, you complain, you have been denied all these; no crown has ever been given you. Not so. Keats would remind us:

> The crown of these
> Is made of love and friendship, and sits high
> Upon the forehead of humanity.

Wear it like a true king or queen!

Suggested Bible Reading: *Matthew 27:27-38*

Prayer:
We come to thee in prayer, O God, wondering at our own temerity and boldness when we call thee Father. We wonder because we realize there have been times when we have been so selective about calling our fellow beings sisters and brothers.

When we come to look so closely at our relationships in the human family, help us to look again at the way we uphold the integrity and dignity of that family. May the elementary lessons we learned as children—lessons in sharing, lessons in showing courtesy, lessons in manners —be brought out again. May these same family lessons be applied in neighborhood, town, and city as we share space in neighborhoods, schools, swimming pools, parks, golf courses. May these family courtesies be shown as we demonstrate that we can let someone else be first for a change, that we can take a back seat.

As we seek more understanding for all persons, may we consciously try to be fast to make friends and slow to make enemies, fast to appreciate acts of kindness and slow to feel grudges, fast to sympathize with weaknesses and failings and slow to criticize, to find fault, and to suspect.

Confirm and strengthen our resolve as we make this prayer, our Father. Amen.

LENT

There was an old organ at home. Built before the days of electronic organs, it worked with man power—plenty of it—supplied by the feet.

Above the keyboard was the usual row of stops bearing some familiar and some [to us] quite incomprehensible names like "Flute," "Trumpet," "Diapason," "Octave Coupler," "Voix Celeste," and others. Naturally, we tried them individually and then in every combination. We always liked the Octave Coupler. There was some fun, almost magic in it—press one key and down along the keyboard other keys went down and played automatically.

Underneath the keyboard were two winglike devices which, when pressed outward by the knees, increased the volume. This may have been our equivalent of present day kids' penchant for turning the stereo up full blast. However, because of our small size and limited dexterity, this posed certain problems.

The thing that probably delighted us most of all (getting music out of the instrument was somewhat secondary!) was to pull out all the stops. This became a two-kid operation. An extra had to get down under the keyboard and help with the pumping, and it had to be fast pumping too because with everything wide open the organ took a lot of air.

That's rather like the Lenten season in the church— we pull out all the stops! The extra volume, the extra effort, the variety of things moving, and the octave coupler effect all suggest ways in which Lent in the church parallels this little organ illustration. Lent is the time when we try harder and renew our commitment to Christ and the church.

Suggested Bible Reading: *Luke 22:1-38*

Prayer:
Christ of ———————— *streets,*
          (your town)
Christ of Palestine,
Christ of revelation:
We come to thee in prayer, we worship thee, we love thee, we try to serve thee. As we watch thee ousting the old and establishing the new, we applaud thee. When we realize that thy revelation is a revolution, we vote for thy way. Then as we observe thee stooping to serve, to help, and to heal, we bend not only our knees but also our backs. Accept our fealty, we pray. Amen.

CONFESSION

The ignorant are brought to knowledge,
the blind to sight,
the desperate to salvation,
the presumptuous to humility,
the troubled to quietness,
the sorrowful to joy,
the sick unto health,
the dead unto life.

The above benefits, as the results of confession, seem to us to be rather extravagant. They are noted by Thomas Bacon in his *Potacion of Lent* (1542). Confession has long been a prelude to the Lenten season. When penance was prescribed, it offered opportunity for regret of sin, acknowledgment of offense to God, and determination to make amendment.

Some of this may seem rather strange to us, for confession is not prescribed or formal in some churches. Likewise, penance is neither regulated nor spelled out in terms of time or quantity. Our carelessness over these matters may not have been to our credit. Many of us would have been living much fuller Christian lives if we had taken opportunity to have God's grace, mercy, and goodness spelled out to us, not to mention if we had taken time to thoroughly renounce some of our faults and failings.

Because we have heard of some of the abuses that grew up under a system of formal confession, such as excommunication, lengthy separation from the church, and flogging, we tend to ignore it altogether.

So during this penitential season, whether we confess our sins privately to God or seek out an understanding Christian friend, a leader of the church, or a pastor, we are doing something of value. Many a person could be saved from compounding error, from making a scapegoat of others, from adding to shame and guilt by use of this essentially practical habit of the church.

Suggested Bible Reading: *I John 1*
Prayer:
We come to thee our Father to make our confession of truth not told, love not shared, gossip not stopped, help withheld, and for all other faults that have become so habitual we no longer notice them. And now we pray not only that we will be forgiven, but that we can accept the relationship which this experience brings. Amen.

FAIR DEALING

Ride a cock-hoss to Banbury Cross
To see a fine lady. . . .

In the lines of the nursery rhyme above, do you know
what Banbury Cross refers to? It is quite an elaborately
built cross located near the town center.

During medieval times markets and fairs were held in
connection with religious festivals. Places of worship
were also places of barter and trade, since shops as we
know them today did not exist.

Sometime during this development from the occasional
market and fair to the shop open for business every day,
appeared the market cross of the type referred to above.
In English towns and even cities such as Banbury and
Chichester these crosses, which may be mounted on a
kind of cupola or have a base with a circular seat around
it, have been preserved.

Many people seeing them today do not realize the connection they have with marketing that took place hundreds
of years ago. The market cross was set up simply as a
sign that here people could buy and sell; it was a symbol
of fair dealing.

Strange, isn't it, the way in which some things change
their meaning? If there were ever a symbol of dirty dealing,
surely the cross was that symbol—particularly the cross
of Christ. Symbols are thought of as having permanent

and universal meaning, but here we see one transformed by an event from "foul dealing" to "fair dealing."

In looking back on the event, we see that perfidy and violence came crashing down as effective ways of conducting human relationships. The crucifixion event teaches us that for all time fidelity and nonviolence have final sway. "Cross my heart and hope to die," says the irreverent child wanting to press home a shaky point. Perhaps the sentiment should be looked at a second time!

Suggested Bible Reading: *Mark 15:21-39*

Prayer:
We pray, O God, for peace—personal and world peace. May our prayers help us clarify in our own minds the understanding that is necessary for us to conquer the conditions which breed wars. We know already that maintaining peace demands more than a white flag for truce, more than signatures on a treaty, more than agreements to stop tests of weapons or commitments toward even more progressive disarmament; but let us be willing to make these moves and then go on to what is necessary in fulfilling them.

For all who are engaged as negotiators of pacts, treaties and agreements, we ask thy blessing. May they be patient in the face of others who are irritated, courageous when called upon to stand for high principles; and may they be farsighted enough to maintain a perspective on what they are saying.

For all who are serving as goodwill ambassadors, we ask thy blessing. Please guide them through their times of success and accomplishment and in their times of loneliness, defeat and opposition. Make them examples of kindness. Let them be humble.

We give thee thanks that there are men and women willing to do these tasks on our behalf. May we be worthy of their expenditure of time and effort. We pledge ourselves to show our concern and our understanding by keeping our families free from excessive strife, by contributing to an atmosphere of goodwill among our work associates, by setting an example of reasonableness and consideration among our neighbors, and by engendering a spirit of cooperation and acceptance for minority groups, members of other races, people from other cultures and countries.

Already we realize that we are undertaking a task too great for our own strength, so we petition thee for assistance through thy Spirit. Amen.

PALM SUNDAY

The King rides in. He comes into the city, his city. People crowd around him, cheer him and follow him in procession. Without a doubt he is a man with a popular and powerful following.

There's something strange about this procession, however; the King is riding a Honda and not a Cadillac with bulletproof dome. Those who run ahead of him on the procession route are making an exaggerated gesture of laying a carpet for him to ride on. Where are the motorcycle police and the security guards?

While the people seem so happy about this whole occasion there's something very restrained about the King. He's not shouting back at the people or waving in excitement. In fact someone said that when he came to the place in the road where he caught his first glimpse of the city— his city—he bowed his head, and they saw tears in his eyes. Strange. You would have expected him to gesture toward it in elation and speak with pride of having conquered it.

Perhaps, as you read this imaginary and fictitious account, you have been thinking a little about the event we know as the triumphal entry of Christ into Jerusalem. What we are trying to emphasize above is the fact that Christ came as no ordinary man, acted in no ordinary way, and received no ordinary response. There was something "extra-ordinary" about everything he did. That is why people were and still are attracted to him. We celebrate the event mentioned above on Palm Sunday. It is also a day when many make a commitment to follow him and his way of life.

Suggested Bible Reading: *John 12:12-19*

Prayer:
(Pull the palms from the trees, wave the fronds, shake them. This is a big day, a happy, jump-for-joy occasion. Let's get together, we can all shout the same thing.)

God, we are happy for occasions like this when everyone can get together, enjoy something they can all understand, have fun without calculating cost or consequence.
(I want a closer, clearer, less cluttered view. Who is this being, small now, so insignificant, so meek, so unassuming, so lacking in command? Why are the people so strangely drawn to him? Why am I so strangely drawn to him, attracted by him, impressed by him? Why is he so confident?)

At the height of our enjoyment, we praise thee, Father, for sending one among us like Jesus—for the fact that Jesus could fit so many roles, that he attracts so many types of persons.
(This man's path should be cleared. Let him pass, speed

40

him on his way, facilitate his journey!)

*Thy truth moves us, O God, and moves on. We stop;
it goes. We are content; it leads to other objectives, other
goals. Keep us from stopping, keep us in step, keep leading; we fall so far behind. Amen.*

SENSITIVITY

It was not more than half a mile from the home where I had spent about twenty years of my life, but I had never discovered it. That didn't mean I had never been on that steep, inaccessible hillside before, but on previous occasions I had been looking for other things.

On this visit I had become interested in fossils—just as a layman, mind you, for I have little idea of what I am seeing apart from the shells and ferns I can readily identify. From past visits to the area I could remember sitting on a rock and noting a variety of fossils embedded in it. Now I was back there really looking for them, and, to my surprise, I came across a huge cliff face one hundred feet or more in height and over two hundred feet across literally covered with a great variety of fossils.

Perhaps this was not a great or valuable discovery (except to me) because there are plenty of other fossil deposits to keep scientists interested. The surprise was that I should have lived so long in the vicinity of this phenomenon in New Zealand's South Island and not known about it. Here was something laid down probably forty to fifty million years ago and during the course of time had been tilted from a horizontal position to an almost vertical one. It is now exposed to the elements in such a fashion that in a few hundred years its part of the record of the earth's history will be lost.

Again and again I come across things like this that make me realize the limit of human awareness. This may be a limit of interest, a limit of useful knowledge, a limit of introspection (so that a person never really understands himself). One of the facets of the gospel is to bring about keener perception, understanding, or sensitivity. We all need it; our too frequently drab lives need filling with fresh insight, fresh facts—even if they are gleaned from a fossil bed as we marvel at God's creation and attempt to understand what was going on thousands of generations before we happened along.

Suggested Bible Reading: *Genesis 1:1-2:4*
Prayer:

> *God, whose glory fills the universe,*
> *We offer thee the thought of our minds, the service*
> *of our hands,*
> *That our worship may be acceptable*
> *And that through it we may discover thy will and*
> *do it. Amen.*

IDEAS

"Ever thought of writin' YOUR life story, Andy?"
"I'd love to, Chalky—"
(There's a pause in the conversation as these two cartoon characters stroll down the sidewalk and then Andy Capp goes on)
"But, I can't remember it."

Since Andy is such a droll character, Smythe, the cartoonist, doesn't even put an exclamation at the end of that speech. After the cartoon appeared I read about one of six conferences for ministers in which the headline said, "Clergymen told to take a Moratorium on New Ideas—Take a Sun Bath—for God's Sake."

Take a moratorium on almost everything else, but on new ideas, never! When we put away ideas for a rainy day, we risk ending up the way Andy Capp did—forgetting them.

True, we can't use every new, untried, screwball, crazy idea that comes to us. We can't be using so many new ideas that people become confused; but the trouble with most of us is that we have so few good new ideas that we are rarely in that danger. Frankly, I feel guilty when I don't share ideas and then find I lose them.

That reminds me of something from Girl Scouts, U.S.A.

When you think you're looking wide, look wider still.
Behold the world that lies outside your window sill!

44

All creation from the start becomes a wonderland
For all who learn to lend a heart before they lend a
   hand!
And when you've looked the world around,
Then look once more, and find the friendship
To be found beyond your door.
You will walk the earth with pride and never look
   your fill,
When you look, and look wide, and look wider still!

Suggested Bible Reading: *I Corinthians 12:4-11*

Prayer:
*Our prayer today, O God, is one of thanksgiving for
thy many gifts to the human race. We pray in appreciation
for our individual endowment, thanking thee for the
uniqueness of our appearance and abilities.*

*Help us in giving words of encouragement to those
whose attitude makes us aware that they feel deprived of
some talent we possess. Keep us ever alert to the special
abilities others have developed; may we never withhold
appreciation because of jealousy or fear of being over-
shadowed.*

*We pray in the name of the one whose talents were
multitudinous and whose use of them for the benefit of
other human beings was unlimited—even Jesus Christ
our Lord. Amen.*

INVOLVEMENT

He was a full-grown man walking in and out of a changing room with a pair of trousers in his hand. There didn't seem to be anything drastically wrong, but he had a worried look on his face. Soon the tailor sensed what was wrong with him and answered his unspoken request—"If you go inside the room and shut the door, the light will come on!"

If you go inside the room and shut the door, the light will come on. Sometimes the exercises that seem impossible, that seem to be the exact opposite of sense, get the job done. Let's look at some of these situations. A broken arm or leg sometimes causes us more bother getting it back into commission again because it becomes stiff in the process of healing. The business of exercising it can at first cause fear that it will be broken again and that the whole process will have to be started all over. Later, it just causes us pain and then more pain, as we stretch it to the point where it can function normally once more.

There are real lessons to be learned here in the world of physical ills, but spiritual and psychological ones fall into a similar category. You sometimes have to shut the door on the past before the light can shine in on the present. You sometimes have to turn your back on a bad habit completely before you can get any light for a new way of living. You sometimes have to cut yourself off from other light sources completely in order to get the switch to activate and throw new light on the situation. This happens when a young person leaves home for the first time. Only through a risk-taking process can he come to gain the confidence and self-assurance and independence that will enable him to carve out a life for himself.

I guess the man in the changing room found that what the tailor said was true. We heard no complaints from behind the door once it was fully closed. Similarly in life, many times when a person has crossed a certain threshold completely, he is content; he no longer fusses about; he gets away from the confusion—even embarrassment—of not quite knowing what to do. "If you go inside the room and shut the door, the light will come on!"

Suggested Bible Reading: *Acts 26:1-32*

Prayer:
God of all:
  May those who came to worship go with added happiness;
  May those who came with fear and doubt go with new faith;
  May those who came in sorrow leave with joy; and
  May those who came to receive go to serve. Amen.

STEWARDSHIP

ONE OF OUR MEMBERS HAD HIS BOX OF OFFERING ENVELOPES STOLEN!

Yes, that's no joke, his car was broken into and among other things, his church offering envelopes were stolen. A person without church offering envelopes could mean a weak spot in our church support, but not in this case, because the man came right in to bring his pledge up-to-date.

ONE OF OUR MEMBERS HAD HER PURSE STOLEN!

That's no joke either. Not only did it make for a great deal of personal inconvenience and anxiety, but it could also have meant a temporary weak spot in the support of our church.

ONE OF OUR MEMBERS HAD HIS WILL TO GIVE STOLEN!

That to us is perhaps the most serious matter of all. He came in here and in a burst of willingness and enthusiasm made his commitment to Christ and in so doing pledged himself to the support of Christ's way—in other words, the church. But, in this case, no one broke into his car or his home and removed something tangible. Just as surely, however, his interest was stolen and his concern was stolen, though the thief was identified by the strange name Rival Interests.

WE PRINT THE STORIES OF THESE BURGLARIES TO WARN OTHER MEMBERS!

For your own protection, to be safe from the third kind of burglary, stay very close to the church. It will continue to teach you ways to stay out of danger.

Suggested Bible Reading: *Luke 16:1-13*

Prayer:
Father of all, who can understand us better than we understand ourselves; help us this day to take a new look at ourselves and in so doing help us to realize afresh thy plan for us. May we live our whole lives as if unto thee, may we seek to increase our usefulness day by day, and may we find joy in serving thee. Amen.

PARTICIPATION

After a rather long, soft passage in the first movement of Tchaikovsky's *Pathetique* Symphony, there arrives a crashing chord that sends everyone bolt upright in their seats. Everything has been going along *pianissimo* when, all of a sudden, it seems as if a torrent has been loosed— an earthquake, an avalanche, a deluge of some kind— and it's back to the orchestra where now the cymbals, the piccolo, the basses, the horns, and even that clown the bassoon are in action, not to mention the tuba.

There are times when everyone in a church is mobilized; 100 percent cooperation is given, everyone is tuned up, everybody plays. Lay participants, speakers, church school teachers, visitors—all are needed. The church has goals to reach, a world to win and serve. United it can achieve objectives and do the will of God.

Suggested Bible Reading: *II Corinthians 9:6-15*

Prayer:
O God, we acknowledge thy gifts of sunshine and rain, rich soil and fertile seed; and we gratefully draw on thy stockpile of marble, granite, gold, oil, coal, ore, uranium and the hundreds of other things that make our life full, productive and free. Help us to give generously of ourselves in time, talent and possessions. When we give generously bless us with a clear sense of having used rightly something we could have abused. Amen.

TITHING

Have you seen a parakeet work an electronic calculator? I have. The bird's owner told me it could, but being of a rather skeptical turn of mind, I hardly believed it until he let the bird out of its cage, flicked the "on" switch and invited it to go to work.

It was really no work to that bird. It pecked on an assortment of keys, and the apppropriate figures appeared in the display. The bird was delighted and continued the game. It showed no sign of having heart failure or apoplexy because an answer indicated a disastrous state of the bird's bank account. The bird continued to peck up a storm [of numbers]. After all, it wasn't developing a headache because of the complicated mathematical problem it was trying to solve.

Pocket calculators have fascinated me. They fascinated me when people talked about the revolution they would bring. They were a curiosity when they were expensive and very limited in capacity. They still fascinate me now that their capacity has been greatly expanded and they are in a lower price range. Evidently they fascinate birds, too!

What is there on the market, intended to do mathematical calculation, which can be turned upside down and used to spell—to spell profound things like S-H-E-L-L O-I-L? Try this problem: 1 divided by 81. It gives you 1234567 whether you want that big an answer or not.

Divide 1 by 9, and then hit the "equal" button twice and see what you get.

These little calculators are so fascinating. I recommend, if you don't have one already, that you rush right out and buy one. If you do, be sure to get one with a percent key on it. You'll need it for the calculation I'm about to suggest.

> Now put your annual salary on the display. (Those figures look pretty, don't they?)
>
> Next hit the "X" and enter 10.
>
> Next press the percent key and the equal sign.

Do you know you have just done something biblical with an electronic calculator that Moses could never have thought of? Now, take that final figure, record it, and begin paying it in weekly, monthly, quarterly or annual installments as your pledge to the church. You have begun doing something Christian with your money!

Suggested Bible Reading: *II Corinthians 8:1-9*

Prayer:
O God, keep us from easy satisfaction with comfortable goals. So often we realize our striving fails to measure up to that of an ambitious person of the world who seeks to do good for the praise it will bring. We come to thee knowing that thy love will send us back to our fellow beings with new concern. In the name of thy Son we pray. Amen.

TRY AGAIN

For almost an hour I had been checking out a meter that did not want to function. After carefully checking all the steps in wiring the circuit, I could find no errors, so I began testing it for continuity, step by step. Everything seemed to be in order.

As you realize, I am no expert in these matters, but just the same, I don't like to have elementary electronic circuits get the better of me. Back I went over all the components like the leads, the power supply, the connections, and still there seemed no reason for that meter to sit on zero as if it were stuck. Then I discovered why no power was getting to it. When the case had been molded, some of the material had run down inside one of the contacts, not enough to show or to block the holes, but more than enough to stop any current from getting through. Now it was simple to clean that material out, and the meter worked!

Ordinary people in ordinary tasks sometimes have to persist to get results. Sometimes it is good for us to realize that some of the "greats" had to persevere, too. Here's an example of one who had to suffer through days of apparent failure when it seemed that he already had success.

Puccini, after his opera *Madame Butterfly* was badly received at its premiere, was so upset that he stayed in his house for two weeks. He wouldn't go out or see anyone. He had visualized the little Japanese girl as he wrote the opera and felt sure that the music would give the same impression of his vision to his audiences. Instead, they complained during the performance because parts of it resembled *La Boheme,* and they cried out "Give us something new!"

Today this poignant opera as performed by most of the major opera companies is accepted and loved by opera-goers, but parts of the original had to be rewritten or modified. Even with a successful work behind him, and regardless of the fact that he had been engrossed in his creation, had given a great deal of time to it, and felt it had real merit, Puccini had not been assured of instant success.

If at first you don't succeed, try, try again! The knowledge that many of the successes around us are the result of people making second, third, and fourth tries is sometimes all it takes to make us dig in and try again.

Suggested Bible Reading: *Ephesians 6:10-24*

Prayer:
O God:
From our world of worry and strife we call on thee.
From the ills of mind and body we pray for relief.

54

*From the gnawing of uncertainty of the future, deliver
    us to thoughts of hope.*
*We rejoice in, celebrate, and experience with gratitude
    —painless and happy days,
    encouragement received and tasks achieved,
    work to do, friends to love,
    loads to lift, hope to share. Amen.*

KNOWLEDGE vs. FACTS

At a boy's reform camp I was once leading some Bible study sessions and, as part of the course, presented the boys with a fairly simple quiz on a variety of Bible questions. The reason for giving the quiz was to learn more about their background in this subject. It would have been futile to talk right over their heads and it would have been just as foolish to underestimate their knowledge completely. Some of their answers surprised me. Their store of information was better than I expected since they were not from churchgoing families and perhaps could be excused for not having had much contact with the Bible at all.

After I had tabulated the quiz, I decided to give it to a group of regular church youth. The age of the two groups was similar. Was I ever in for a surprise when I compared the results of the two groups. Our good, wholesome, law-abiding, church- and church-school attending kids knew little if any more about the Bible than those boys in the state reform institution!

Now before going any farther, let me point out that the quality of answers was pretty poor in both cases. Perhaps there was more reason to be shocked over the infinitesimal amount of religious knowledge the church-related youth had retained. However, that was not the pearl I was trying to glean just now. What strikes me again and again is the conclusion that the possession of a head full of facts—good facts, Bible facts, knowledge of salvation—is far from a guarantee that a person will put them to a good use. Is it possible to assume a person will put them to any use at all unless properly motivated? In more recent years Christian educators have attempted to take the emphasis off rote learning of facts and have attempted to make the learning process person-centered.

Suggested Bible Reading: *Luke 10:25-37*

Prayer:
"May the words of our mouths" be governed by a care and concern for individuals within our range of influence, and may "the meditation of our hearts" be marked by an increased understanding of thy truth, "O Lord, our strength and our redeemer." Amen.

COMMITMENT

The work detail of natives was gathered in the cleared area of the jungle and heard the plantation owner recite particulars of the job they were to do in preparing for a crop to be planted. It was hot, the work was tiring, and the plantation owner had to go on to supervise another work detail elsewhere. Past experiences had taught him that the minute he left the clearing and was out of sight, the natives would slacken their pace and soon find a shady tree under which they would rest until they heard him returning.

While the natives were still gathered round listening to his instructions, the plantation owner made a very pointed ritual of removing his glass eye and placing it on a stump in the center of the cleared area. Banking on their ignorance and superstition, he let them know it would watch them until he returned.

He left and they, while casting furtive glances in the direction of the glass eye, went to work. Presently, as the heat became more oppressive, one of the bolder ones in the group started crawling on hands and knees in the direction of the stump. He deliberately kept below the level of the eye. At a distance of a few feet he took off his hat and with a deft toss threw it on top of the stump covering the eye. Tools were dropped and the whole group headed for the shade.

The plantation owner, anticipating some hanky-panky, had remained hidden some distance from the group. Here was an unfortunate development, but he was not easily foxed. He raised his rifle with its silencer attached, took aim at the offending hat and shot it clear off the stump. The effect of this new magic was immediate, powerful, and permanent. The natives went back to work and did not down their tools again until the plantation owner returned.

This is a scene from a story I read while in my teens. I remember neither the title nor the author. This part of it comes back to me whenever churches contemplate peoples' response to stewardship commitment.

There is a tendency to think that a hat has been dropped neatly over the all-seeing-eye by saying, "I don't believe in pledging." Everyone knows they don't, their tools are down and they are lounging in the shade! Some feel they have covered the penetrating eye by saying, "What a person gives is between him and God." Some think they have shut off the line of sight by stating, "The Church is always asking for money."

Perhaps we waste too many words trying to convey what a New Testament writer said so pointedly, "No one makes a fool of God."

Suggested Bible Reading: *Matthew 28:16-20*

59

Prayer:

*Lord, we ask thee for courage to put away any tempta-
tion to withhold our resources from thy service. Make
us realize more fully that we will always lack something
until we put our whole life at thy disposal.*

*Light up the small duties of our daily life that we
may know glory dwells in the commonest task. Help us
to work as if we are all the time directly in thy service.*

*Take from us the despondency that comes when we feel
that in many ways we fail thee. Give us joy in service
and hope that in future we may overcome our failures
and make life a success in thy sight. Amen.*

RELIGION: REAL OR ?

A male hitchhiker perched fairly comfortably on a guard rail at the entrance to an interstate, caught my attention. It was not his appearance, or dress, or stance that caught my attention, but something he had in his hand. Now we are used to hitchhikers who carry signs naming their hoped-for destination, others who obviously attract the attention of the motorist because of their uniform, their interesting looks, or simply their beaming smile.

Sunday's paper carried a cartoon of one hitchhiker holding a sign reading, "Whither thou goest, I will go!" But the hitchhiker I am speaking of may have gone one better than that because he was holding a Bible in his hand. He was holding it rather ostentatiously, shall we say, as if he was about to open it and read, but at the same time did not want to take his attention off the traffic.

Since I was riding alone in another direction I had time to reflect on what was in store for any person who picked him up. Would it be Philip and the Ethiopian eunuch situation in reverse? Would it be a free sermon or exposition for some person who did or did not want to hear more about the Bible? Or, on the other hand, was the Bible just being held there as a means to a free ride somewhere?

Perhaps one of you picked up this young man and can answer the question that remains in my mind, or perhaps answer it in part. Are religion, the Bible, Christianity just a means to an end? How many more questions this evokes:

Is this a fair use of the Bible?

Would a genuine Christian ever do this kind of thing?

Why not tell another Christian that I am a Christian out on the road waiting for a ride, that I will live by this Bible and do him no harm!

Was it really a Bible or did it just look like one?

When the young man put the Bible in his sack, would he pull out a gun?

Frankly, I have yet to form an opinion of whether this use of the Bible was legitimate or not, but I remain suspicious. Have you formed an opinion pro or con, or are you suspicious, too?

Suggested Bible Reading: *Acts 8:26-40*

Prayer:
Lord, help us to understand that if we are to be anything before thee, we may have to be nothing before men. If we are to be great in thy kingdom, we may have to be a servant in this world. Help us to serve.

May the reversal of values for thy sake fire us with a true spirit and avoid a perversion which repulses the world instead of attracting it for thee. Amen.

MISTAKES

What do you do when you make a boo-boo, or have a memory lapse?

Arthur Schnabel, famous concert pianist, used to play long, involved piano solos without a note of music in front of him. I stand in awe of anyone who can play "Jingle Bells" note perfect, let alone a Beethoven piano concerto.

Well, eventually it happened, as these things do. In one concert, Schnabel had a complete lapse of memory— he didn't just forget a couple of notes, his mind went blank and he stopped completely. It also happened that a woman in the audience had a copy of the music open on her lap—she was following as he played. Schnabel got up from the piano, walked across to where she was sitting, quietly asked if he could borrow the music, looked at it briefly, handed it back to her and went back to playing without further ado.

The lady was more flustered than Schnabel. The rest of the audience paid no particular attention and the music critics never mentioned it. Schnabel took this situation for what it was and handled it like a pro.

Not everyone has this kind of aplomb. We are reminded of it by a clip that appeared in the *Christian Caller* from First Christian Church, Auburn, Indiana. It said an editor explained away his mistakes this way, "If you find errors, please consider that they appear for the benefit of those readers who always look for them. We try to print something for everybody."

Our editor is another example of a pro! How do you handle your errors? Correct them quietly, bluster and try to make someone else look foolish, call everyone's attention to them and so make them ten times worse, blame someone else, especially someone who will have a hard time defending himself? These are all ways of dealing with a boo-boo. Everyone makes mistakes. It is how we get around them that counts.

Suggested Bible Reading: *James 3*

Prayer:
O God:
Thou whose secret is with the reverent: save us from intellectual pride either of attainment or failure. We would see things steadily and as a whole. We would be wise yet modest. Teach us our failings and faults. Lift us above the unstable currents of self-will. If the shadows deepen, bring us an awareness of the resources around and within us. May thy spirit dwell in us more and more. Amen.

AUTOMATION

When school starts in the Fall, students in large, city schools spend time getting courses straightened out that have suffered due to the over-zealous, erratic, or stupid computer. Now computers, as we know, break down and malfunction; but we suffer from their vagaries more because of operator error than mechanical or electronic failure. In the meantime the computers can be blamed as if they really did make mistakes; but when they begin to laugh, then we will be in real trouble!

Goober on the "Andy Griffith Show" was computer matched in a date with a psychiatrist. He had invalidated his application by checking that he read thirty books a week—comic books, that is, and other similar literature. No machine has ever been made that can take over our responsibility to think as a human being—to reason sensibly or to ask sensible questions if we expect sensible answers. As long as computers are made so that they can just spit out million dollar checks when we press a button too many times, we're not in too much long-term trouble; but when they laugh at our mistakes, then we will be really embarrassed.

One computer was reported to have put an $18.5 million rocket in a wobble course so that it had to be destroyed. Analysis of what caused this situation showed that a hyphen in the computer program was missing.

In a world where we have been able to make machines do many of our boring tasks, we still have to live as human beings. We can sometimes get away with blaming another human for our mistakes because he is willing to accept the blame; a machine will not.

Most of us come into this picture, not at the point of receiving a check that is one hundred times bigger than it should be, but at the point of putting up with the inconvenience, embarrassment, or injustice that occurs because someone punched the wrong button and caused us to be billed for something we didn't buy, to be denied credit for a bill we paid, to be deprived of our welfare check, or to be confused with another person whose name is the same. There is no point in thumbing our noses at the machine, nor in hammering its transistors to fragments; it will neither cry nor bleed. In each succeeding age, as life becomes more and more complicated, man will inevitably be forced back to his best ethical and spiritual resources, all of which are found in Christianity in sentiments like:

> Hate will never work.
> Love will always work—ultimately.
> Selfishness destroys.
> Sacrifice can do wonders.
> Justice is not enough.
> Freedom must be used; it can't be stored.

Knowing and applying these things enables us to live with our mistakes and laugh at our own foibles, but if ever computers begin to laugh at us, then we will know we are in real trouble.

Suggested Bible Reading: *Matthew 6:1-18*

Prayer:

> *O Thou whose days are not numbered,*
>> *whose faculties are never lost and never fail,*
>>> *whose faults are not compounded,*

Hear our prayer, O God. Give us patience to bear up on days that never seem to end. Make us understanding when we look back on life and find either that it has been too short or we have been prodigal with time we have had. Let us derive full value from the ministries of love found in a sweet smile, a gentle touch, a pleasant voice or any extension of these in deeds of love. Help us by thy spirit to share thy word with our words and deeds. Help us also to share thy work by our willingness to sacrifice. We pray through—

> *The one whose days were numbered,*
>> *whose facility was limited by our humanness,*
>>> *even the Lord Jesus Christ.*   *Amen.*

AUTOGRAPHS

Autographs are sometimes fascinating. They can be a clue to the size and stature of the person who gives them. Some of them are frivolous, some are pointed and sharp like a rapier.

Though the former fashion of toting an autograph book and plying all celebrities with it seems to have faded, the custom persists in the form of autographed pictures, programs, and books. As you might have guessed, I am about to quote a few of the autographs I have remembered across the years! It would be possible to dredge down into the memory and come forth with quite a pile of them, but really there are only a few (besides the frequently used quotations from great literature) that have stayed with me.

The school teacher who taught me most during my grade school years used this one, "To err is human, to forgive divine." It took me some years to realize this may have been a profound comment on her experience with me as a pupil—and not the other way around! Another one used over and over by a youth director was six simple words, "The best is yet to be."

Well, each in its own way suggests a bit of mirth, a wryness, a stab to alertness, a spur to accomplishment. This is a folkway that goes back a very long way—at least as far as Confucius.

A famous man was asked what his motto in life was.

He replied, "No virture in easy victory." A motto like this is only as significant as the person it represents. Could you guess whose motto this was? It might have been a person who had spent his life struggling against intolerable or insurmountable physical handicap. It might have been a person who hunted for big problems to solve and worked on them. In fact, it was said by Sir Edmund Hillary, conqueror of Mt. Everest.

A story is told of a mountaineer who disappeared into the clouds on a mountain, reappeared in a clearing, then was seen no more. When last seen he was still climbing.

What is your motto? How do you write an autograph?

Suggested Bible Reading: *Matthew 5:1-16*

Prayer:
"Lead us not into temptation," O God, because we realize how vulnerable we are. Here are some of the things with which we need help:

> *the temptation of flaunting our power to avoid certain habits and yet leading others into a danger zone;*
> *the temptation of underestimating our talents and so depriving thee of glory;*
> *the temptation of overestimating ourselves so that we alienate fellow beings and make them see us as insufferable;*
> *the temptation to underrate thy power to love, to change, and to continue with us to the end. Amen.*

LIVING

"Life is a lot like a tube of toothpaste. You always have to squeeze hard to get the most out of it."

This bit of wisdom appeared on Burton Hillis's page in *Better Home and Gardens* magazine (June 1971). Come to think of it, some people may be getting very little out of existence because they haven't found the right place to squeeze.

Life is a lot like a tube of toothpaste—and some squeeze so hard the tube ruptures.

Someone bought a new car and was plagued by a constant rattle in a door. He kept pestering his dealer and getting it examined, tightened, oiled, and still the aggravating noise continued. Finally he prevailed on a mechanic to take it apart. Inside he found a coke bottle, and inside the bottle was a note which read, "I wondered how long it would take you to find this!" Some try to squeeze so much out of life—they maybe squeeze too hard.

Life is a lot like a tube of toothpaste—some squeeze it in the middle, some roll it up neatly from the end, some just squeeze it anywhere.

Did you realize that getting something out of life may be far less important than the way you go at it? Your own way, your personal way, your unique way of expressing yourself as an individual is important.

Life is a lot like a tube of toothpaste—once it is squeezed out, it can never be put in again!

This is a thought many of us need to keep in mind. Squeeze out only as much of life as you need for the occasion, for the day. Now we will vary our approach to this little parable by saying, unlike the tube of toothpaste, life needs the cap left off. Be ready for the experiences of life all the time.

Suggested Bible Reading: *John 10:1-21*

Prayer:
Expand our consciousness of life, O God, for we are awed by its complexity, overjoyed by its wonder, and thrilled by its variety. May all of this make us more willing to face life in imaginative ways, more resilient in times of great hardship, more realistic about justice and love.

Permit us to balance what is beautiful with what is unlovely. Against hunger, pain, frustration, or boredom, let us match moments of joy, tenderness, and fulfillment.

Preserve us from the trap of complete satisfaction with this world as it is. May we be dissatisfied enough to keep searching for a new world, a more complete world, the only perfect world in thy kingdom. Amen.

ANGER

"You don't seem to be mad at anyone, Coach," remarked the interviewer.

"No," replied the Coach, "I'm not paid enough to get mad at anyone!"

Do you know what this man was really saying? Was he making an innuendo about the size of his salary? Or was he really saying he couldn't be paid enough to get mad at anyone? In either case it raises some other questions.

Who, and how many people can you afford to get mad at? Can you really afford to get mad at anyone? If you get mad at bad people, as some would recommend, what good is it? What about getting mad at bad deeds? Will that change them?

It would be our natural expectation that with its emphasis on love, tolerance, acceptance, and other such things, Christianity would put emphasis on not getting mad at all. It doesn't. Well, not in every case.

A very noteworthy passage is written in the Bible on the assumption that we will all get mad sometime, at someone or some thing. The twist in the approach is that it suggests how to deal with our anger once it exists. Perhaps the best time to remind ourselves that we should take steps to limit the effects of anger is at times like this when we are not mad at anyone. Here is the passage I referred to, Ephesians 4:26 in *Today's English Version of the New Testament:* "If you become angry, do not let your anger lead you into sin; and do not stay angry all day."

Suggested Bible Reading: *Mark 11:15-18*

Prayer:
Lord, save me from the stupidity of others—from the irrational, thoughtless, irritating, inconsiderate acts that plague me on my off days and sometimes make me almost unbearably angry. Keep me first of all from spilling out my anger on others who have done nothing to deserve it. In the second place, keep me from venting it on those who have deliberately or inadvertently caused it, since they are probably not going to benefit much or change much because of it. Thirdly, save me from destroying myself with it.

Now that I have said all this I can settle down and thank thee for the fact that there is more to existence than petty human happenings. It also amazes me that by being calm I can find so many ways around obstacles that seem insurmountable, troubles that seem unending. Amen.

ILLUSIONS

What, in God's Name? This simple expression can be understood when spoken, but misunderstood when written. When heard, the inflection tells whether it is blasphemy or inquiry. We use it despite its illusionary quality.

Carl Haas tells a story about Henry Eccles, a musician. Though not well known, Eccles was competent and talented. At some point in his career, however, he became a Quaker and took up shoemaking. With his new found religious enthusiasm he went to extremes. He burned his music, he burned his musical instrument, he condemned "steeple houses" (church buildings), and he even demonstrated in London churches. On two consecutive Sundays he insisted on entering the pulpit and making shoes! He was forcibly evicted. He also stripped to the waist and "semistreaked" the London streets.

Another such comment that may make us reexamine what we do and why we do it is the statement: "Most Christians tend to worship their work, to work at their play, and play with their worship." *What, in God's Name?*

Suggested Bible Reading: *Isaiah 30:6-11*

Prayer:
O God, who art the truth: teach us step by step what we do not know, preserve in us that which we do know, correct us when mistaken, strengthen us when we fail, and deliver us from all that is false. Amen.

WORK

People have various ways of knowing when to quit at the end of the day. What's yours?

Is it when you feel too tired to go on?
Is it when the last customer has left?
Is it when the boss or supervisor has left?
Is it when you have finished the particular task you started?
Is it when the boss tells you to leave?
Is it when you have completed a certain number of hours?
Is it when the whistle blows?
Is it when you are bored and want to do something else?

Now that you have picked out the way or ways you finish your day's work, is it the right way for you and should it be the right way for everyone else? The way we quit our work at the end of a prescribed period, probably has a great deal to say about us! It may reveal our motive for working or what we are getting out of our work; or perhaps it indicates our attitude toward life.

Jackie Mason, in one of his jokes says, "One of the first jobs I ever had was really ridiculous. For eight hours a day I did nothing. The only problem was that I never knew when I was through."

This discussion is not intended to make you so introspective about your work that you become unhappy with it, but to make you see it for what it is and then hopefully to encourage you to make it more meaningful and, perhaps, more satisfying.

The following two prayers have a bearing on the issue we are trying to get at here. One is for use before work, the other after work is over.

> There are only eight hours in this work day—
> God, help me to use them well. Amen.

> Bless the work I have done today, O God. May it achieve something for the general good rather than use up a block of time as easily spent fishing or fooling around. Amen.

Suggested Bible Reading: *Galations 6:1-10*

Prayer:
Father of all mankind, we humbly thank thee for the freedom of choice that enables us to make up our minds. Teach us to rely on thee for guidance in making the decisions that will determine our lifelong goals. Give us a clear vision of the difference between the good life and the bad, between truth and falsehood. May we never foolishly place ourselves under temptation with the mistaken impression that we are testing our strength. Show us our weakness so that we may know how much we need to depend on thee. Amen.

FRIENDSHIP

"Do you have many friends?"

"No."

"How about acquaintances?"

"Yes, but you wouldn't call them really good friends."

"Do you feel any need for good friends?"

"Yes, but I don't want to get so involved with neighbors that we spend all our time together."

Several people may recognize themselves in the conversation above because it has been constructed from a number of different incidents.

The need for significant, lasting, and deep friendships has never been greater than it is at the present time, yet many things stand in the path of cultivating and keeping friends today. People with young families do not have the time to join in activities with adults their age. People with busy schedules can't spend the time cultivating friends. Often there isn't enough money left to entertain friends. Some become inhibited about making deep friendships because people are so often on the move and no sooner begin a friendship than one or the other moves away.

One reason people do not make more permanent friendships today may be that they are involved with so many groups of acquaintances—for example, neighbors, co-workers, fellow PTA, golf club, bridge club, and church members, and maybe a dozen others. Except in small towns these sets of casual acquaintenances consist of different people. Knowing many people a little satisfies some persons because they feel there is less danger of a "falling-out," less likelihood of the relationship wearing thin, less chance of exposing personal weaknesses and failings.

Charles Schultz introduced many of us to his "Peanuts" characters with a book titled, *I Need All The Friends I Can Get!* That is perhaps the first step in remedying the situation we have been describing—a recognition of our need and a deliberate attempt to change selected acquaintances into friends.

This process of selection is one of the very important elements of forming friendships. It may be easier for the person who has one consuming passion in his life—say stock car racing—than for the one who has twenty-five different interests and hobbies. The one who has many interests has to select friends who are compatible with several of them. Maybe one clue to cultivating acquaintances is to concentrate one's interest in particular subjects or activities.

Shakespeare spoke of friends and acquaintances in *Hamlet:*

> Those friends thou hast, and their adoption tried,
> Grapple them to thy soul with hoops of steel;

But do not dull thy palm with entertainment
Of each new-hatch'd unfledged comrade.

Suggested Bible Reading: *Luke 11:5-10*

Prayer:
Create in us a deep and abiding love for our friends as we realize how much they add to our lives, O God. May we seek to cultivate in our lives those qualities of trust and dependability that will enable us to make friendships that will endure throughout life.

Let us live above petty disappointment when our friends do not measure up to our high expectations. Help us to make attractive to them qualities which will enable them to do better.

May our chief friendship be with thee. Once again we place our confidence in thee. We ask thee to be patient with us in our selfishness, stupidity and shortsightedness. Bear with us in our weak efforts to improve and help us to realize that thy grace is sufficient reward for our striving. Amen.

79

WORSHIP

> They who are content to remain in the valley
> will not see the grander view from
> the mountaintop.

So goes an intriguing quotation and so goes life!
  There's the alarm clock shock.
  There's a bill collector at the door.
  There's a death in the family.
  There's a week of work.
  There's five o'clock freedom.
  There's joyful payday.
  There's the final payment on the house.
  There's a weekend of relaxation.
Some of these things come and go, and there is little we can do either to prevent or preserve them. There are other things in life, however, available to us if we put on our climbing boots, as the quotation above suggests.

Much of the drudgery, the routine, the sameness, the boredom of life can be relieved if we know where and when to seek relief. Some of the drabbest lives I know are lived by people who week after week deny themselves the mountaintop view of life that can be obtained from the experience of worship on Sunday.

Sure it may require some effort to pull on the climbing boots; it may strain some muscles to climb the steep slopes of the mountains of inspiration; but who can deny that there is the reward of the grander view from the mountain-top?

Remember to go to church on Sunday.

Suggested Bible Reading: *Mark 9:2-13*

Prayer:
We come before thee, O God, to bring our offering of worship, praying that it may be an acceptable gift of our love and devotion.

Help us when we come to worship with a sense of fatigue to be alert enough for the encounter of truth with error and relaxed enough to appreciate thy peace which passes understanding. Calm us when we come with so much energy that we find the tempo dull. Be especially close when we come to worship because we feel it is expected of us and would rather be somewhere else. Direct our thoughts to something of value. Bless us with the clear understanding that we will receive strength and renewal from thee. Amen.

AFFECTION

"It's already been pushed once," the lady explained as we rode down in the elevator. To say that here doesn't make much sense, but in the elevator it meant the woman had already pushed the button for the floor at which I wished to exit, so there was no need to repeat the action. As I left the building I mused on her statement because I have often simply watched as people pushed the same elevator button several times rather than bother to explain that it had already been pushed. But that wasn't all; I began remembering the impatient ones who stand outside an elevator and push the button twice, three times—sometimes pumping it about half a dozen times—in their impatience to get an elevator to come faster! This is rather amusing because the machine shares neither their enthusiasm nor their annoyance. Perhaps they remember the days when an evelator operator was called by a buzzer. Sometimes he wandered off and couldn't hear it. Of course, there are still a few operators, and perhaps the riders think they have come across a particularly lazy one. Could they be thinking on the other hand that the modern automatic elevator is run by some sleepy person at the top of the elevator shaft!

These are all thoughts instigated by some person's chance remark, but there was something I actually said in response to the lady. After thanking her for her information, I commented, "Many of us wish people were like these elevators and only had to be told once to do exactly what we want." You might see the list that follows as a series of buttons designed to get action.

"Get off dead center!"
"Get moving."
"Pass the bread, please."
"Will you please help me?"

Each one can be repeated with varying emphases—such as: "GET OFF DEAD CENTER!"—to make it take effect. With human beings, repetition of a request for action is sometimes necessary, but with a good machine, once is enough.

In the family that moves with the precision of clockwork on a nine-ulcer schedule this machine-type response is desirable, even essential. How do you make it work? On a machine you supply power, keep it adjusted and oil the points of friction. Does this follow with the human in a family? Food, clothing, sleep, medical care may be thought of as the essential ingredients, but they only go so far.

Sometimes we seem to make our worst blunders when we act on the assumption that among human beings we can get by with those things physical and material. "Man does not live by bread alone" was said long enough ago and been demonstrated enough times to be considered

a self-evident truth. Some character thought this statement was incomplete and added, "He needs cake as well."
Not so. He needs understanding, affection, appreciation,
discipline, prompting. You may think I am rattling these
things off as if they are easy things to give. Quite the
contrary. To give these consistently and in the right
quantity to the members of our families is about the
hardest thing to do. More power to those who are trying
to do so.

Suggested Bible Reading: *Luke 4:1-13*

Prayer:
*God, I pray that my life may be lived as a son/daughter
rather than as a prodigal. Help me to appreciate the value
of home and to discount the lure of the far country that
would lead me to swinish living.*

    *Father, with thy discipline teach me to be an obedient
child. Be my guide to things true, good, and beautiful,
and keep loving me even when I do not deserve to be
loved. Amen.*

CHURCH ATTENDANCE—A JOY

A young boy was crying, and his father was taking him home. The child had not misbehaved; quite the contrary, as far as we know, he had been exemplary. The boy was crying because he just didn't want to leave church and go home; he had been having such a wonderful time!

Whenever we hear of an event like that we want to pass it on because we feel that too often people fail to share the values and the joys and the help they derive from belonging to the church, from associating with other Christians, and from taking time to worship. Does it make sense that we take trouble to keep our church school fully staffed with teachers who are competent, concerned for their students, consistent in their attendance, and always in their classroom before the first student arrives? Does it not strike a familiar chord to be very concerned that our classrooms be clean, painted in pleasing colors, equipped with first-rate equipment, up-to-date, and therefore a pleasure to use?

If in the future we find whole families crying because they have to leave church and go home, we'll consider that something good is going on at church.

Suggested Bible Reading: *Ephesians 1:15-23*

Prayer:

Father, we come to thee yielding our spirits to thy direction.

We thank thee for thy church because it makes us feel stronger when we are torn with grief and do not know where to turn for support because life has tumbled in upon us.

We thank thee for thy church because it gives us the opportunity to share our strength while we are healthy, strong, and self-reliant.

We thank thee for thy church because it gives us guidance when we are young, immature, and uncertain.

We thank thee for thy church because it gives us a sense of security when we grow old and look behind to see others following, others lifting us when we cannot walk alone, and others taking our place.

For this day and through this week we ask the blessings of self-assurance, ready speech, and understanding for those who live the Christian message, asking people to commit their lives to thy kingdom. We call upon thy Spirit to stir the conscience, enlighten the mind and excite the spirit of all those who join in our endeavors to make the kingdom a reality. Amen.

HUMOR OF GOD

A source of medicines
　　ingredients for fomented drinks
　　　a food supply for cattle and wild animals
　　　　candies
　　　　　preserves
　　　　　　　a water supply for a stranded desert traveler
　　　　　　　a state flower
　　　　　　　a miniature garden
All of these come from one or another of the one thousand varieties of the plant we know as cactus. It so
happens that we do not wish to speak of any of these
things, nor about the fact that some cacti bloom only at
night, that some have such excellent storage systems they
go for two years without water, that cacti have a waxy
covering to retard evaporation and spikes to keep thirsty
animals from chewing on them.

There are the tiny pincushion cactus plants and the
imposing barrel cactus with its symmetrical arrangement
of flowers and dozens more varieties that are interesting;
but it is the giant, sometimes seventy feet tall, *saguaro*
that we want to talk about.

"The God who made *saguaro* cactus must have a sense
of humor," was my comment as I drove through the miles
of arid, hot, seemingly endless desert last summer. Such
weird, such grotesque, such comical shapes are assumed
by these things that your imagination runs riot. A finger,

a whole hand, a nose stuck at a rakish angle, a hat cocked to one side, they are huge, exaggerated, out of proportion. Sometimes they look as if they are alive and could march like soldiers; sometimes they are tipsy and look like a street full of tottering, intoxicated figures. Then there is one that is tall and straight and perfect and you wonder why it is so unlike the others.

Yes, when you can drive a desert highway without feeling danger or discomfort and have time to muse on things like this, you feel that, among other things, God has a sense of humor—a terrific sense of humor!

Suggested Bible Reading: *Psalm 100*

Prayer:
God, we believe in you as the eternal, personal Spirit, creator and upholder of all things. We believe that you are sovereign Lord, exalted above the world, that you order and overrule all things for the accomplishment of your holy, wise, and good purposes.

We believe that you made us to love and serve you, that you care for us as a righteous and compassionate Father, and that nothing can either quench your love or finally defeat your gracious purpose for humanity.

Help us to translate these beliefs into a style of life that reflects the glory of being your daughters and sons. Amen.

CHRISTIAN LIFE

A long-bladed grass scythe hanging on the wall of an antique shop reminded me of earlier days when I made my first attempts to swing one of those cumbersome, sometimes dangerous things. Though there were power mowers then, the kind we had left large patches of grass around the trees in the orchard—hence the need for the back-bending, blister-raising hand implement.

It always seemed possible to take in too much grass or too little grass with the scythe in a swath that should have been neat and clean cut. There was that sharp pointed tip that always wanted to dig in the ground, interrupt the beautiful rhythmic swing, throw you off balance, and sadly affect your dignity [if someone were watching].

But nothing was as odious to the novice hay mower as a blunt blade. That scythe I saw the other day was all rusted over, and not even a master of the art could have made a decent cut with it. Apart from the difficulty of holding the tool in the right position, they never seemed to make child-size handles for the things, and this meant that a youngster trying to sharpen it always tended to come at it with the wrong angle on the sharpening stone. After a time of valiant effort with the wriggling, unsteady tool and the cumbersome sharpening stone, a person would go back to work again. Always it seemed that in that very first swing after you had done an excellent sharpening job, you struck a stray piece of wire or a rock someone had thrown into the field. (I can fully understand why my father and grandfather were so willing and eager that I learn to sharpen the tools I used!)

A scythe, left hanging on the wall, may accumulate some value as an antique, but it will never increase in value as a working tool. In the hands of a person who knows how to swing it, the blade tight in the handle and the small handles adjusted to the right position for the person using it, it becomes a thing of value. Recount some of these things and see the similarity between this situation and that of the Christian life. Hanging on the wall—not much happens; in the hands of a clumsy novice—it's dangerous; blunt—it's annoying and hard to use; out of adjustment—it's inefficient. So, if the analogy is worth anything, all through life keep yourself sharp, keep in adjustment, and above all, stay in use.

Suggested Bible Reading: *Philippians 4:8-13*

Prayer:
O God, keep us from easy satisfaction with comfortable goals. So often we realize our striving fails to measure up to that of an ambitious man of the world who seeks to do good for the praise it will bring him. We come to thee knowing that thy love will send us back to our fellow men with new concern. In the name of thy Son we pray. Amen.

POWER

On the northern tip of South Island in New Zealand is a lighthouse situated at the end of a series of sand dunes. To make a trip out to Farewell Spit Lighthouse it is necessary to travel fifteen miles along the beach between tides. Trucks were once used for the trip, but they were unreliable because there were soft places in the sand where they would mire down. Sometimes when this happened the trucks were abandoned; the tide came up over them, and they were ruined. The modern vehicle has very low gears by which power can be applied to all the wheels. This gives remarkable pulling power and is a great boon.

In place after place in the New Testament, we find allusions to this kind of "pulling gear" that is available to man, ready to help him and keep him from getting mired down. "Believe" is one of the power words Jesus uses: "All things are possible to him who believes" (Mark 9:23 RSV). "Faith" is another one of these power words: "If you have faith . . . nothing will be impossible to you" (Matt. 17:20-21 RSV).

The trip to the lighthouse is a difficult one but it affords scenes of rare beauty: sunrise and sunset, sand formations piled up by wind and tide, rocks, sea shells by the thousand, and, at a certain season, the assembly of godwits and other rare birds about to make their migratory flights. Life can afford us many exciting experiences, and if we make the proper preparation and take reasonable precaution to equip ourselves with sufficient power, we can travel with assurance and safety.

Suggested Bible Reading: *Mark 9:14-29*

Prayer:
Father of our coming and going, we commit ourselves to thee. We appreciate the full provision made by thee to meet our needs. Keep us from trusting too much in our own strength or from forgetting to equip ourselves with the power thou has provided. Amen.

GOD'S PRESENCE

Lord:
I shall be verie busie this day.
I may forget thee
But doe not thou
Forget me.

These words of Sir Jacob Astley's prayer before the Battle of Edge Hill are very familiar to me because I had them in bold lettering on my wall for several years. I suppose Jacob Astley prayed this way in all seriousness, because no doubt he was fighting for his life that day, but I wonder if we have any right to pray that way in the general course of life.

True, we live in a world filled with distractions. It is a busy world and an engrossing world, but should we expect God to give constant care to millions of us when we spare him no more than a passing thought? You might say it is God's nature to concentrate without being distracted, and it is human nature to have the attention divided!

You might even go farther and say that it would be impossible to get any work done if one were thinking about God all day long. Perhaps our attitude to God should be in terms of a pilot and his navigational equipment. One instrument in a small plane is referred to as the VOR. It shows whether the plane is approaching or going away from a radio signal from the ground. By means of variations in a sound signal the pilot can tell if he is moving off course to the left or right. He does not give his whole attention to this device because he has dozens of other things calling for his attention, but he has been trained to respond to that signal as soon as it shows he is drifting off course. He then makes appropriate corrections.

Suggested Bible Reading: *Psalm 121*

Prayer:
> *Lord:*
> *I shall be very busy today.*
> *Enable me to listen to thy signals,*
> *Make necessary corrections,*
> *Stay with the flight plan,*
> *And arrive at my intended destination. Amen.*

CRISIS

In the blacksmith shop there were occasions when my father needed assistance with hot pieces of metal which were taken from the forge and placed on the anvil for welding or beating into shape. The ringing noise of hammer blows, the shower of sparks, the red hot iron, and the jarring force from the hammer made me hold the tongs at arm's length and secure the piece of metal with just enough strength to keep it from falling to the floor.

To a timid boy this jarring from the hammer seemed at times almost to shake my arms off. Noticing this reaction my father would say, "Hold on tightly and then it won't jar you." This seemed contrary to good sense but under the circumstances anything was worth a try. It worked. I found that when the tongs were gripped and the metal held firmly most of the chattering and the jarring ceased.

When in the face of shattering, jarring blows a crisis in life seems to be shaking you to the foundation of your being; remember the advice of the blacksmith, "Hold on tightly." If you happen to be confronted with the loss of your life's savings, are deprived of your means of livelihood, have to face the rest of life with a seemingly intolerable handicap, or have been separated from a loved one, you, too, may feel like the blacksmith's assistant who was inclined to drop the metal and tongs and run.

As soon as you have strength to stand up to the situation at all, remember the words of the blacksmith, "Hold on tightly and then it won't jar you." It works with metal and it works for men.

Suggested Bible Reading: *I Thessalonians 5:12-28*

Prayer:
> *Let us pray to God:*
>> *for patience*
>> *for goodness*
>> *for responsiveness*
>> *for gratitude.*
>
> *Let us pray that God will aid us in our fight:*
>> *against impatience*
>> *against temptation*
>> *against dullness*
>> *against selfishness. Amen*

WINNING OTHERS

"The good shepherd lays down his life for the sheep" (John 10:11).

Our neighbors used to keep sheep. One night I found one in a stream. At the time I had a dog with me and I could have sent him to bark at it. I could have shouted at it myself, or beaten it, but none of these would have been of any avail. The sheep was upside down, caught in a briar, wet and cold. In this condition no amount of harsh treatment or persuasion could make it move. Before long it would have drowned. The only way to save this dispirited animal was to get down in the water and lift it up on to the bank, getting wet and cold in the process. A cold, wet sheep not trying to help itself is a considerable burden, and carrying it back to safety on the bank was a struggle. Even when rescued this sheep showed no sign of appreciation!

Such an experience is like evangelism. We should not delude ourselves into thinking that simple short cuts will save all the lost. Barking at them, beating them, shouting at them, telling them to help themselves, even explaining how it can be done will not always suffice. It takes identification with them, lift, effort, struggle and some- times willingness to undergo danger in order to spiritually move the lost. As Christians we are in this kind of business—winning people to the involvement we want them to have in the kingdom of God.

Suggested Bible Reading: *John 10:7-17*

Prayer:
> *O God, we're inspired, we want to go out and*
> *win them all;*
>> *win many, if we can't win them all;*
>>> *win one.*
> *We know that so often we end up*
> *winning a few or*
>> *winning none.*
> *Why is this so, Lord?*
>> *Are we so weak?*
>>> *Are they so willful?*
> *At least we know it is not your fault. Amen.*

EFFORT

"You've got two hands, why don't you use them?" It's amazing that a person can remember some things for a decade or a quarter of a century or more without writing them down or having them repeated. That's one admonition I remember because at the time I heard it I really should have been using both hands. Employed to grade apples, my boss let me know that I was only giving him half the work he should have been getting for his money, because I was using only one hand. The other hand wasn't broken or tired out, I just hadn't put it to work.

Others have realized the potential of double-handed effort. Some valiant warriors in King David's bodyguard were known for their ambidexterity. "They ranked among the warriors valiant in battle. They carried bows and could sling stones or shoot arrows with the left hand or the right" (I Chron. 12:2 NEB). Not everyone can achieve this kind of thing, but that is not the place where most of us fail. Many times we do not even make an attempt.

God has given us opportunities to make a two-handed success out of life. Help to someone handicapped, words of commendation, telephone calls to a lonely person, letters or visits to someone homebound may be ways of achieving this. These may seem like "one-finger" efforts to some of us, but perhaps it is better to begin on this level than to begin with some grandiose suggestions.

No matter how you construe a two-handed effort, this is a good time to begin. The boss's rather sharp-tongued comment stayed with me and did me a lot of good. "You've got two hands, why don't you use them."

Suggested Bible Reading: *II Timothy 4:1-8*

Prayer:
God, everlasting giver, we never-ending takers thank thee when we walk with arms swinging—every muscle free—along a long, straight, level lane; run and feel dozens of muscles pull, surge forward—uphill against a wind; stand firm against a gale—on a cliff's edge; lie relaxed on a carpet of grass—breeze and sun making perfect comfort; sleep, dream; wake, imagine; think. Thanks God! Amen.

ADVENT

If your nose is close to the grindstone,
   and you keep it down there long enough,
You'll soon forget there are such things
   as the sea, and a brook that babbles, and a
     bird that sings.

Three things then, your whole world will compose:
   yourself, the stone, and your darned old nose.

Advent, if there is to be any time in the years for fun, should be one of the times for getting the nose off the grindstone. If there is any allotted time in the calendar for a change of pace, a new look at life, a time for enjoyment, this is it; for Advent literally means, "an arrival" and marks the beginning of the Christian Year (i.e., the Church's liturgical calendar).

Year after year, in spite of this fact that Advent is a time of joyful change, people complain about not having time to be able to really enjoy it. If we are going to thoroughly exhaust ourselves through trying to do entirely too much, we should at least spare some energy for enjoying the change—the different spirit in people, the decorations, the music and the break in the routine.

As we look toward Christmas let us imagine contrasting attitudes for some of those in the original situation and see how these alternatives sound:

Innkeeper: I didn't get a minute's sleep last night with all those late arrivals; and then that commotion with the guests in the stable capped everything! All I can say is, I hope this never happens again!

or

Innkeeper: That sure was pandemonium last night, but it turned out all right. Here's a refund of your money. Come to the inn again any time. You brought us such joy and excitement you will always be welcome.

Whatever role we choose to play (and within certain limits we do choose) sets the tone, not just for ourselves, but for many who are around us. Advent—enjoy it while you can. It's new, a beginning. It's a time for starting over and doing better than ever before.

Suggested Bible Reading: *Luke 1:26-56*

Prayer:
O God, make this season of Advent a time of enlightenment for us. Help us to know thee as the Holy One, holy and yet helpful. We thank thee that Jesus came to make us more alert to man's likeness to thee. Keep us conscious of thy love for us. Amen.

LOVE, JOY, HOPE, PEACE

The words of advent are: "Love," "Joy," "Hope,"
  "Peace."
  They are words to use in conversation.
  They are words to use in greetings.
  They are words to use in worship.
  They are words to use in Christmas cards.
  They are words to use on decorations.

Now we know there are a lot of other words that get
frequent use at this season: "layaway," "bargain," "sold
out," "bonus," "charge," "rush." You will probably find
occasion to use them too, but we hope you will be at-
taching more importance to the first set of words. They
are ones that are likely to give life a better flavor and
quality.

Suggested Bible Reading: *Matthew 1:18-25*

Prayer:
*O God of love, who didst break into our world by an-
nouncing and entrusting the birth of thy son to a young
woman, help us to accept the fact that thou art breaking
into our world of stolid thoughts and solid things with
wonders almost too great for our understanding.*

Give us wisdom to follow stars of truth as faithfully as we now track satelites and space ships. In days when we shoot men to the moon, let us not overestimate our own prowess and understate the vision of those who responded to the sign that a King of the world was to be born.

Give us the willingness of the shepherds to break out of our mundane routine, stand the risk of taking a loss, and go immediately to where the action is. But let us not mistake a fuss for real action; let us not confuse disturbance or furor with those departures from the hard world that spell compassion, new human sensitivity, broadened tolerance, increased appreciation for difference.

So may the spirit of the Christ child enter our lives as we are willing to put ourselves in the picture, giving clear recognition, giving unstinted adoration, giving our choicest, most precious gifts to him. Then may he cleanse us, renew, and uplift us. Amen.

CHRISTMAS GIVING

We are a very crabby lot.
Nothing suits us long.
If it had been a grand march played,
We'd wish it had been a song!

People crab about the commercialization of Christmas. Christmas lures us into the stores to do a bit of buying for someone else. We may be buying something that could easily be done without, but at least we interrupt our regular pattern of thinking first, second, and always of ourselves.

As a purely commercial event, Christmas keeps a lot of people happy. Usually we think about the store manager with his office door open listening to that glorious song of the jingling cash registers. But there are others who share his joy—from employees who are store clerks to those who manufacture all the different goods we buy. Without Christmas the economy would be a lot more sluggish.

Donald Swann wrote about these things in his book *The Space Between the Bars*. He contended that many of us need some kind of festival like Christmas—spread out over a number of weeks—to put us in the mood for giving. (Usually it's no problem to get people into the mood for receiving.) He also maintained that there is something downright confusing about our giving to those who already have too much. Isn't there some way in which we can attend to more of the ones who don't have enough or don't have anything at all?

When we've bought all there is to buy for the "person who has everything," do we then extend the Christmas spirit to some who have nothing? How about putting someone on your Christmas list this year who has next to nothing?

Suggested Bible Reading: *Matthew 25:31-46*

Prayer:
O God
  of the annunciation,
  of the heraldic angels,
  of the hurrying shepherds,
  of the guiding star,
  of the curious magi,
  of the harmful Herod,
Be thou our God
Even when we know
We are no fit house for thy Spirit.
We let our halos tilt.
We watch clouds not stars.
We look for thrones not stables.

We shun crosses and covet crowns.
Claim us as yours,
O God,
Who at the turn of the era
Came to a proud,
    a possessive
    people.
Claim us as yours. Amen.

PRINCE OF PEACE

CHRISTMAS is a time when we give closer attention to the central figure of history—the Christ. We give a kind of lip service to his remarkable accomplishments, his dynamic personality, and his controversial teachings; but we do very little to put them into practice in our lives or to make those around us do what he taught.

Since Christ's birth is connected with the idea of peace (angels announced "Peace on Earth"), let us examine this. From the moment of his birth, Jesus had enemies. King Herod threatened to kill him—he was an enemy. Later a hostile crowd tried to shove him over a cliff— they were his enemies. Religious leaders plotted his defeat and death—they were his enemies. Judas, one of the twelve disciples assisted in the plot—he was an enemy, too.

Thus Christ lived in the midst of hostility and not in a protected environment where he had no temptation to act aggressively, to lash out at those who threatened him, or get even with his opposition. Yet in this situation, what did he do and what did he teach? "Turn the other cheek," "Go a second mile," "Love those who hate you." These are sayings typical of the calculated kindness, the deliberate, purposeful attack he made on enemies and opposition.

If actions speak louder than words, we need to study what Jesus did. In the case of the crowd threatening to throw him over the cliff, he evaded them; in the case of the religious leaders, he spoke against them with strong language but neither armed himself against them nor encouraged any of his followers to undertake any form of physical violence. He did make a physical attack on the vendors in the temple, but observe that this was directed at their equipment and wares—he did not use the whip across their backs.

From the Prince of Peace we learn to fight wrong doing without destroying those persons who are the enemy or our own best sons. From the Prince of Peace we learn to overcome our enemies with kindness, cooperation, and help rather than preparing to obliterate their loved ones and countrymen, their cities, homes, places of worship, and means of livelihood.

While the Bible can be very vague on some issues, it leaves little room for doubt on this one. It says nothing about Christmas truces, cease-fire agreements, or non-aggression pacts. It does not say to withdraw and let the enemy take over what he wants, or to surrender everything without putting up a fight. Here is one of the things it says, " 'If your enemy is hungry, feed him; if he is thirsty, give him a drink; by doing this you will heap live coals on his head.' . . . Use good to defeat evil" (Rom. 12:20, 21 NEB).

When we keep using goodness only to maintain our friends, a mixture of good and evil to win the uncommitted, and nothing but evil to combat the enemy, what can we expect? Without waiting for the all too painful answer to that one, let us encourage leaders everywhere to use nothing but good to conquer evil.

Suggested Bible Reading: *Luke 2:1-8*

Prayer:
O God, whose son was the Prince of Peace,
May we speed goodwill ambassadors,
 peace corpsmen, and negotiators
 to replace
 soldiers, spies, and snipers.

Make our cargoes of
 food, clothing, and medicine heavy, and
 place permanent embargos on our
 delivery of bombs, bullets, and gas.

Help us respond to cries for help
 soon enough and sensibly enough
 that we no longer are forced onto the defensive,
 nor entice others to be aggressive.

       Amen.

CHRISTMAS GIFTS

Uncle Porkypine in the "Pogo" comic strip came up with a piece of wisdom when he opined, "More folks believe in Santa Claus than believe in Christmas."

Santa Claus is easy to believe in; he represents material gifts.

Christmas is hard to believe in; it represents ideas and attitudes. Now that you see Christmas in that light, are you satisfied with your point of view? Does it seem reasonable to make this kind of distinction? Is it necessary that we pull these two apart and view them as separate? Why not combine the two? Our giving of gifts, symbols, and representations of ourselves should flow from our ideas and attitudes concerning both people and things.

What do you think the cave man gave his friends? Smooth or shiny rocks, a shell with delicate colors or striking shape, a bird's feather or an egg, a drawing on a piece of bark or slate? At least we can conclude these were the things he had around him. He lacked the brightly colored wrappings, the ribbons and bows, the musical boxes and bells; but in all likelihood his gifts were as carefully chosen and as deeply appreciated.

Man undoubtedly gave gifts before Christmas ever came about and would have continued giving gifts had it not happened. What then did the event of Christmas confer on this giving situation that was not there previously? We conclude that it drew attention to the per-

111

sonal nature of giving and relating to people. You can limit the cost of gifts to twenty-five cents or remove all restrictions by saying exchange can amount to a million dollars or more, but the Christmas idea is not so much to give the superlative gift as to give self in a superlative way—to love, stand beside, support, encourage, help another, or many others. This may involve a gift or it may not; what is behind the gift is what counts.

Suggested Bible Reading: *Luke 2:8-20*

Prayer:
Bless, O Lord, those families that will not be united this Christmas—whether because of war,

> *service,*
> *conscience,*
> *travel,*
> *mission,*
> *quarrels,*
> *distance,*
> *money.*

Heighten the joy
> *for all who have planned and waited and longed for this festival.*

May it truly unite us with each other
> *and with the holy family.*

Bring to us
> *an inexhaustable desire for peace. Amen.*